# Everybody Digs Soil

# MICRO LIFE IN SOIL

## Natalie Hyde

 Crabtree Publishing Company

www.crabtreebooks.com

# Crabtree Publishing Company
www.crabtreebooks.com

**Author:** Natalie Hyde
**Editor-in-Chief:** Lionel Bender
**Editor:** Lynn Peppas
**Project coordinator:** Kathy Middleton
**Photo research:** Susannah Jayes
**Designer:** Ben White
**Production coordinator:** Ken Wright
**Production:** Kim Richardson
**Prepress technician:** Ken Wright
**Print coordinator:** Katherine Berti

**Consultant:** Heather L. Montgomery, children's writer, environmental educator, and science education consultant who runs Dragonfly Programs: http://www.dragonflyeeprograms.com

**Cover**: Every handful of soil is packed with organisms or living things.
**Title page**: A section through soil, showing an earthworm

This book was produced for Crabtree Publishing Company by Bender Richardson White.

**Photographs and reproductions:**
© FLPA: title page and pages 18/19 (Derek Middleton), 7 right (Rosemary Mayer), 18 (Nigel Cattlin), 22/23 (D Jones), 23 (Nigel Cattlin)
© Getty Images: pages 4 (Geoff Brightling), 5 left (Kim Taylor), 13 (Dr. David Phillips), 15 left (Photolibrary), 15 right (Wally Eberhart), 17 left (Wim van Egmond), 20 (Maria Stenzel), 21 left (Darlyne A. Murawski), 28 (Noel Hendrickson), 28/29 (John Howard), 29 (Jupiterimages)
© iStockphoto.com: Headline image (redmal), pages: 6 (jeridu), 7 left (Edward Brubaker), 11 left (Janice Hazeldine), 11 right (David Andrén), 12 (Mike Sonnenberg), 13 left (Dongfan Wang), 14 (Hans Laubel), 17 right (Nancy Nehring), 19 (Pattie Calfy), 21 right, 22 (Ana Maria Rincon), 25/25 (Steve McWilliam)
© JLP/Jose Luis Pelaez/Corbis: cover (girl and plant)
© www.shutterstock.com: cover (all except girl and plant), pages 5 right (Bidouze Stéphane), 8 (Neale Cousland), 9 right (Tischenko Irina), 10 (LockStockBob), 16 (Attila Jándi), 24 (Scott T Slattery), 25 (Koshevnyk), 26 (Richard Griffin), 27 left (AnutkaT), 27 right (Mary Terriberry)

**Library and Archives Canada Cataloguing in Publication**

Hyde, Natalie, 1963-
    Micro life in soil / Natalie Hyde.

(Everybody digs soil)
Includes index.
ISBN 978-0-7787-5402-2 (bound).--ISBN 978-0-7787-5415-2 (pbk.)

    1. Soil microbiology--Juvenile literature.  2. Microorganisms --Juvenile literature.  I. Title.  II. Series: Everybody digs soil

QR111.H93 2010          j579'.1757          C2009-906274-7

**Library of Congress Cataloging-in-Publication Data**

Hyde, Natalie, 1963-
Micro life in soil / Natalie Hyde.
    p. cm. --  (Everybody digs soil)
Includes index.
ISBN 978-0-7787-5402-2 (reinforced lib. bdg. : alk. paper)
    -- ISBN 978-0-7787-5415-2 (pbk. : alk. paper)
1.  Soil microbiology--Juvenile literature. 2.  Microorganisms--Juvenile literature. I. Title.
    QR111.H93 2010
    579'.1757--dc22
                                                2009042781

## Crabtree Publishing Company
www.crabtreebooks.com          1-800-387-7650

Printed in the U.S.A./012014/SN20131105

**Published in Canada**
**Crabtree Publishing**
616 Welland Ave.
St. Catharines, Ontario
L2M 5V6

**Published in the United States**
**Crabtree Publishing**
PMB 59051
350 Fifth Avenue, 59th Floor
New York, New York 10118

**Published in the United Kingdom**
**Crabtree Publishing**
Maritime House
Basin Road North, Hove
BN41 1WR

**Published in Australia**
**Crabtree Publishing**
3 Charles Street
Coburg North
VIC, 3058

# CONTENTS

# A PLACE TO LIVE

**S**oil is not a pile of crushed rock and dead leaves. Every handful is packed with organisms, or living things.

### A SMALL WORLD

"Micro" means very small. Some of the **organisms** in soil are so tiny they are invisible to the naked eye. A microscope is needed to study them. They include **bacteria** and **fungi**. Others are visible but still small. Among these are many kinds of worms and insects. Together these organisms are known as "micro life."

▶ *Slugs, snails, and many insects move on the surface of soil. Many kinds of worms and grubs burrow through soil.*

## THE IDEAL HOME

✳ Soil is an ideal place to live. It is rich in **nutrients**, including water and oxygen, which almost all living things need.

✳ Buried in the soil, or under stones or fallen leaves on the soil's surface, living things can stay cool and safe from enemies.

✳ In soil there are places to build homes and nests for young, store food, and keep out of the heat, dryness, or cold.

✳ Trillions of creatures of all kinds live in soil.

## UNDERGROUND NURSERY

Earwig mothers are very protective. They build a special nest in soil for their eggs. They lay about thirty eggs at once. Mothers look after their eggs all winter by sealing themselves inside the nest. Then they lick their eggs over and over to keep them clean.

## CICADA SYMPHONY

Cicadas are large colorful insects that can be heard in the summer. Their singing sounds a little like an electric saw. Cicada eggs are laid in twigs and when the **larvae** hatch they fall to the ground. They **burrow** down in the soil and live by sucking fluids from plant roots. Some cicada larvae live underground for 17 years before turning into an adults.

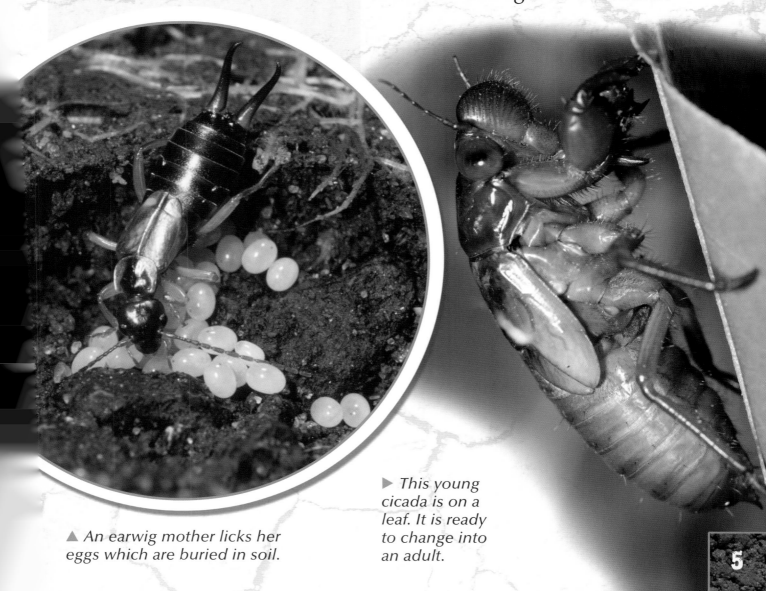

▲ An earwig mother licks her eggs which are buried in soil.

▶ This young cicada is on a leaf. It is ready to change into an adult.

# LIVING UNDER GROUND

Organisms that live in soil are adapted, or built, for life under ground. Their sizes and shapes make it easy for them to move through soil material. They have senses to help them find food and escape enemies in a dark, silent world.

## SENSING THE SOIL

Soil is made up mostly of particles, or small pieces, of rock, as well as dead animal and plant material. Most soil organisms are very small and can easily move between soil particles. With no sunlight under ground, most soil micro life depend on their senses of hearing, taste, touch, and temperature—not sight. Earthworms, for example, sense **vibrations** in the ground to help them find their way.

▶ Young ants grow within soil and, as adults, help turn fallen leaves into nutrients.

*Allgood Elementary School*

A

*▲ A millipede crawls through leaf litter and crumbs of soil.*

## LOTS OF LEGS

Millipedes are worm-like organisms with many body segments, or parts, that bend. Each segment has two pairs of short legs. Millipedes can have from just 11 to hundreds of segments and up to 750 legs. Their legs and bodies move like a wave, and this makes it easy for them to burrow into the soil.

## SOIL LAYERS

✳ Different layers of soil have different organisms living there. The top few inches are home to **microbes** like bacteria and fungi. Ants and earthworms move farther down into the soil. Larger animals such as mice and moles tunnel deep into soil.

*▶ At a landslide, you can see the layers of soil with rock underneath.*

# DECOMPOSITION

Decomposition is the way materials are recycled in the soil. It means breaking down organic materials into chemicals that plants can use again.

## WHO IS AT WORK?

When a squirrel dies and falls to the ground or a tree sheds its leaves, the squirrel's dead body and leaf litter are soon attacked. Birds, shrews, insects, spiders, and mites pull them apart. Ants, termites, slugs, worms, and millipedes break down the material more. Bacteria and fungi get to work, releasing all kinds of nutrients and **chemicals** into the soil. Plants use these nutrients to grow and reproduce.

◀ These fungi take their nutrients from trees.

▶ A view of bacteria seen through a microscope

# FOOD CHAIN

**1.** *Clover grows using energy from the Sun and minerals and chemicals from the soil.*

**2.** *Grasshoppers eat clover. They are herbivores or plant-eaters.*

**3.** *Toads are carnivores. They eat grasshoppers. They catch them with their sticky tongues.*

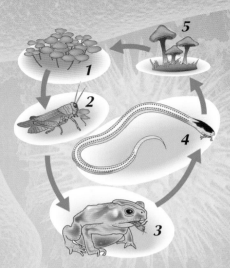

**5.** *Toadstools and microbes break down organic matter like snakeskins into chemicals and* **minerals**.

**4.** *Garter snakes eat toads. Garter snakes shed their skin three or four times a year.*

A food chain shows how each living thing gets its food. Plants make their own food using nutrients from the soil and energy from the Sun. Some animals eat plants. They are called herbivores. Carnivores are animals that eat other animals. Humans are omnivores because we eat both plants and animals. Plants, which grow in soil, are at the beginning of the food chain.

## SOIL FACTS

✳ Fungi and bacteria feed on organic matter in the soil. They are an important link in the food chain.

*Allgood Elementary School*

**A**

9

# MUSHROOM MADNESS

Fungi are not plants or animals. They do not make their own food as plants do, or kill and eat other living things for food like animals. Fungi get their nutrients and energy from dead and decaying, or rotting, matter.

## HOW DO THEY GET NUTRIENTS?

Fungi include molds, yeasts, puffballs, mushrooms, and toadstools. They are called decomposers. They release chemicals, known as **enzymes**, that break down dead animals and plants, then take up the nutrients released. Fungi do not need sunlight to make food as plants do. They can grow in dark places such as caves, tunnels, or in the soil.

## MARVELOUS MOLDS

Molds usually grow into large groups or **colonies**. They work at breaking down sugary chemicals called starches. Some molds give off chemicals that kill other organisms. This leaves more food for them. Scientists discovered that doctors could use these chemicals to make medicines that can kill bacteria that cause diseases in people.

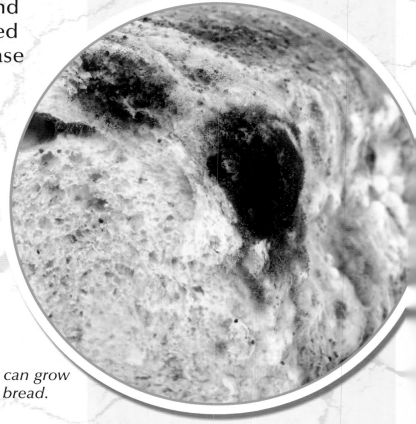

▶ Molds can grow on stale bread.

## TOUGH STUFF

Cellulose is the tough fiber in plants. It is very hard to break down or digest. Even humans cannot digest it. Fungi use enzymes to break down the cellulose. This releases chemicals containing carbon into the soil. All organic material has carbon.

## SPREADING OUT

Some soil fungi produce long, hair-like threads called **hyphae**. The hyphae join together under ground to create what looks like spiders' webs. The webs keep the soil together and help hold in rainwater. This way, nutrients are not washed away too quickly.

▶ *Toadstools are, like mushrooms and puffballs, the reproductive parts of fungi. They are a mass of hyphae that grow out of the soil.*

# BILLIONS OF BACTERIA

**B**acteria were some of the first forms of life on Earth. They have been around for 3.5 billion years.

## GAS-FIXERS

Bacteria are microscopic, one-celled organisms. An ounce (28 g) of soil contains millions of bacteria. Most bacteria in soil are decomposers. Others can take gases out of the air and turn them into nutrients. This is known as gas-fixation. Nitrogen is a gas that is vital for plants. They need it to make **proteins** for cell growth and repair. Nitrogen-fixing bacteria make plant nutrients from nitrogen in air.

◄ *Bacteria are so small they must be viewed with a microscope.*

## AERATION

✱ Air is a mix of gases including oxygen, nitrogen, and carbon dioxide. Bacteria need air. Getting fresh air into soil is known as aeration. This happens naturally by the action of soil animals.

## BACTERIA FACTS

✳ Bacteria are shaped like balls, rods, or spirals. Some have little hair-like structures called pili. These allow them to stick to things. They can cling together to make a cluster or stick to other surfaces.

✳ If all the bacteria died, every living thing on Earth would die, too.

✳ There are so many kinds of bacteria that scientists have been unable to name all of them.

## CHEMICAL DIET

Chemotrophs are special bacteria. They get their energy from chemicals and not from the Sun or by breaking down organic material. Some of these bacteria live near volcanoes, or on the ocean floor, as well as in soil. They feed on ammonia and chemicals containing sulfur. Other chemotrophs feed on **pollutants** such as pesticides, which are chemicals some farmers use to kill plant pests.

## CELL FACTS

✳ A **cell** is a building block of life. Microbes are made of just one cell. Larger creatures are made up of many cells working together. Humans have trillions of cells.

▶ *A magnified view of threadlike bacterial cells*

# PLANT PARTNERS

**P**lants depend on micro life in the soil. Some help aerate, or bring fresh air, into soil. A few fight plant diseases. Some micro life bring minerals or chemicals that plants cannot get for themselves.

## BETTER TOGETHER

Scientists have discovered that plants grow better with certain bacteria and fungi in the soil. The microbes and the plants work together so they both benefit. This is called a **symbiotic** relationship. When plants in different fields are compared, the ones with more microbes in the soil are much bigger and healthier.

## YOU DIG IT

Grow some bean plants from seed. Place some of the young plants in pots filled with garden soil and others with houseplant soil. Put the pots on a sunny window ledge indoors. Which plants grow best?

▶ *A scientist checks how well plants are growing.*

# NETWORKING

Root fungi grow near the root systems of plants. They take sugars from the plants for food. In return they provide the plants with nutrients. Each root fungus forms a large network of threads. The threads reach out through the soil much farther than the plant's roots. This means the fungus can bring nutrients and water that the plant cannot reach.

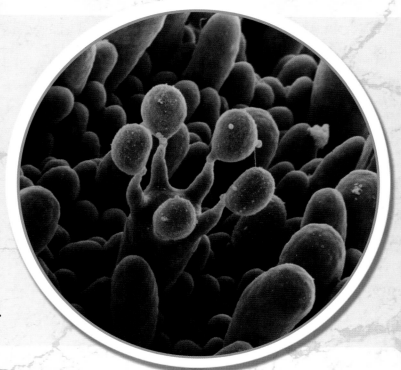

## LUMPS AND BUMPS

Rhizobia are a type of soil bacteria. They are one of the nitrogen-fixers. These bacteria enter the roots of **leguminous** plants, which include peas, beans, soy, and clover. This causes a small infection. The plant creates a nodule, or bump, around the infection. This is where the bacteria live. They provide the plant with nitrogen, and the plant is a source of food for the bacteria.

▶ *Root nodules on a leguminous plant*

# TINY ANIMALS

Protozoa are one-celled animals. They live in ponds, lakes, the seas, and in the soil. Protozoa come in many shapes and sizes. They have different ways of moving and eating.

## WHAT DO THEY DO?

**Protozoa** in soil usually live near the root systems of plants. They feed on bacteria. As they do, they release extra nutrients into the soil. At the same time, they can kill bacteria that may cause diseases in plants.

## LIVING TOGETHER

Some protozoa live in other soil animals. Termites cannot digest wood on their own. Protozoa living in their gut help break down tough fibers. Once they are broken down, the termites can digest the nutrients.

*Allgood Elementary School*

▶ *A termite colony lives in the soil and in a mound it builds above it.*

## SHAPE SHIFTERS

Amoebas are a type of protozoa. Some amoebas live in the mud at the bottom of ponds. They have a unique way of moving. They move by stretching a part of themselves forward. It looks like a foot. Then they pull the rest of themselves along. They also use this shape-shifting to eat. When they find a meal, they stretch out their sides to surround it. The amoebas use enzymes to digest what is trapped inside.

▶ An amoeba has surrounded some food.

## SWIMMING ALONG

✳ A paramecium is a protozoan common in pools of water that collect in leaf litter. Some paramecia have green algae that live inside. The algae provide oxygen for the paramecia which, in return, provide protection. Paramecia eat bacteria, algae, and yeasts, keeping soil healthy.

▶ A close-up view of a paramecium in water

# EARTH EATERS

One of the heroes of soil is the earthworm. This simple creature plays many roles in the health of life under ground. The earthworm's diet helps create new and fertile soils. The tunnels it makes lets air into packed soil.

## GOING DOWN?

Earthworms drag plant food down into their burrows. Grass, leaves, and petals are moved from the soil surface down under ground. Earthworms do this over and over. They are like miniature earth **tillers**. This spreads organic matter through soil so organisms and plants can reach them more readily.

## LEFT BEHIND

Earthworms feed on microbes in the soil. They also eat organic materials such as leaves and stems. The food is ground up inside the earthworm. When it has **absorbed** all the nutrients it needs, the earthworm pushes the unwanted material out of its body. These are worm castings. They contain many nutrients and inorganic chemicals. Worm castings are what make the soil **fertile** or good for plant growth.

▲ *Worm castings on the surface of grass*

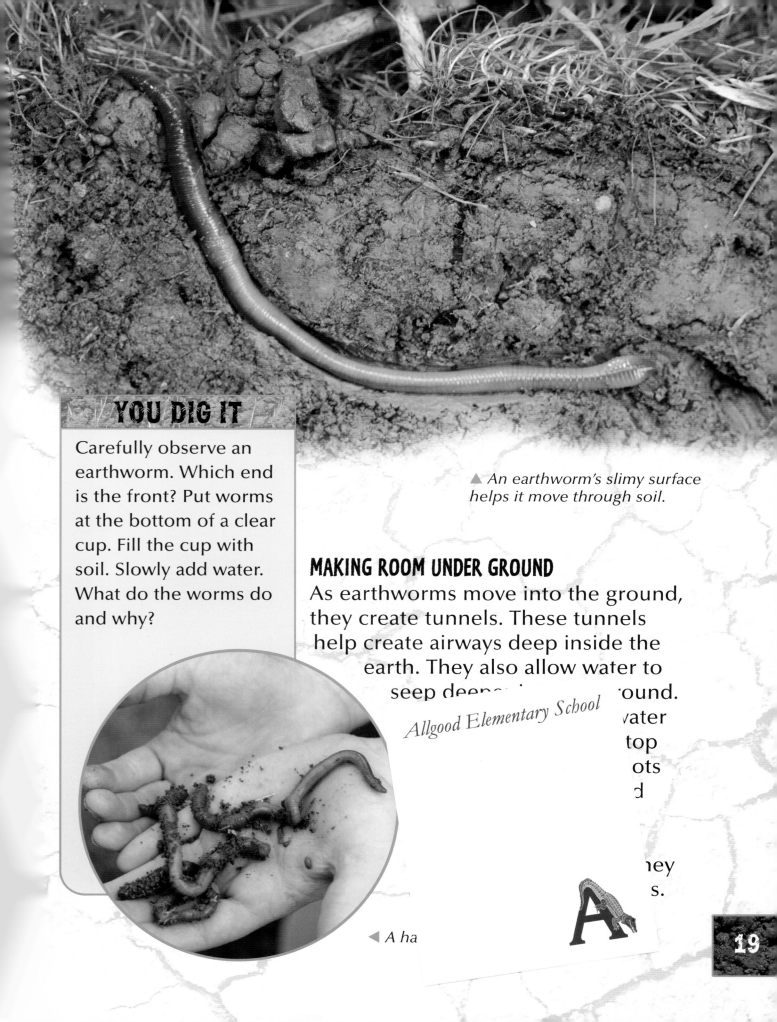

_▲ An earthworm's slimy surface helps it move through soil._

## MAKING ROOM UNDER GROUND

As earthworms move into the ground, they create tunnels. These tunnels help create airways deep inside the earth. They also allow water to seep deep___ _____ _____ound.

_Allgood Elementary School_

vater
top
ots
d

ney
s.

◀ _A ha_

**A**

19

# THREADS OF LIFE

**N**ematodes are threadlike microscopic worms. They have more than one cell, so they are multi-celled creatures. They are also transparent. This means you can see right through them.

## WHAT DO THEY DO?

Like other micro life, nematodes help release nutrients into the soil. When they eat bacteria, they leave behind chemicals for plants to absorb. Nematodes also help spread microbes through the soil. Some bacteria and fungi hitch a ride on their bodies.

▼ Nematodes in soil are badly affected by **global warming**. Each year scientists check nematode numbers in identical areas of soil to see how they have changed.

## WHAT'S FOR DINNER?

Different types of nematodes eat different things. Some eat bacteria or fungi. Others eat protozoa or even other nematodes. Eating a variety of organisms is important because it releases a range of nutrients into the soil. Nematodes help balance the types of life forms in the soil.

▲ Nematodes are vital micro life in the soil of a garden.

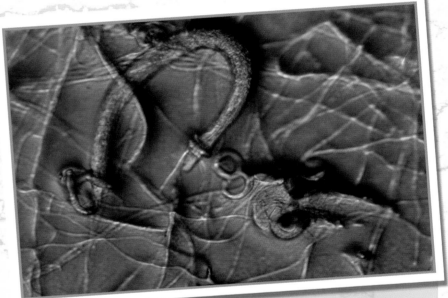

▲ Nematodes and hyphae

## NEMATODE HUNTERS

Some nematodes are harmful. They can cause diseases in plants and animals. Certain types of soil fungi trap nematodes. One kind lays out sticky hyphae that capture nematodes moving through soil particles. Another fungus makes knots in its hyphae that it can tighten around the nematode.

## WORM FACTS

✳ There are more nematodes in soil than any other multi-celled creature on Earth.

✳ Nematodes live in almost every type of soil.

✳ Nematodes live mostly on roots and the moisture on soil particles.

# JOINTED LEGS

**A**rthropod means "legs with joints." This group of organisms includes ants, mites, millipedes, spiders, and sowbugs. Many are part of soil micro life.

## SHREDDERS AND PREDATORS

Arthropods that eat dead plant material are called shredders. They shred dead leaves, stems, and flowers to feed on the fungi and bacteria within and on them. This helps break down larger pieces of organic material into smaller ones. Millipedes are strong shredders. Spiders, centipedes, ants, scorpions, and termites are predators. A predator hunts other animals. These types of arthropods usually have strong jaws to kill and cut up their prey.

## YOU DIG IT

Set up a light above a wire or cloth screen full of soil. Put a bucket of water under the screen. Leave overnight and observe all of the creatures driven out of the soil by the light and heat.

▲ *A spider in the soil*

▲ *Soil mites*

◄ *A pseudoscorpion on the prowl*

## MIGHTY MITES

Mites in soil can be shredders or predators. Under a microscope, they look like a mini helmet with legs. Predator mites pick on smaller creatures. They will attack springtails or even the eggs of insects. This type of mite has a long pointed mouthpart.

## GETTING AROUND

The springtail gets it name from the way it moves. It has a forked tail that works like a spring. When it is under attack, it pushes off and jumps around the soil. A springtail can jump up to twenty times its own length. Springtails eat bacteria and fungi around the roots of plants. They keep down the number of harmful organisms so plants are not damaged.

## ARTHROPOD FACTS

Arthropods do not have a backbone. They are protected by a hard outer shell. They feed on both plants and animals.

# WASTE-PROVIDERS

The top few inches of soil in a forest or grassy field have been recycled many times. Every piece of soil has been through the guts of many different organisms.

## LEFTOVERS

The waste from different organisms helps the soil in different ways. Springtails and silverfish scrape fungi off roots and eat them. They need only some of the nutrients in their food. The rest is pushed out. Other organisms use the waste as a source of food.

## SOIL FACTS

✳ Some animals, including humans, have bacteria in their guts. As organic matter passes through their digestive systems, the bacteria mixes with the waste. Organic-waste fertilizers spread bacteria over the soil.

▲ Millipedes are good organic-waste providers. They eat dead plant stems, roots, leaves, and bark. Their waste is particularly rich in nutrients.

## ROLY-POLYS

Pill bugs, or sow bugs, like to live in damp places. They are found under logs or in manure, the waste from cows and horses. Shell-like plates protect their bodies. When they are in danger, they roll into little balls.

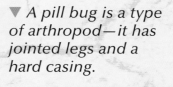

▼ *A pill bug is a type of arthropod—it has jointed legs and a hard casing.*

## YOU DIG IT

Lay a loop of string on the ground. Have each player put one roly-poly in the middle of the loop. The roly-poly that crawls to the string first wins. Without touching your creature, can you do anything to affect its race and make it the winner?

▲ *A mole cricket*

## MOLE CRICKETS

Mole crickets are excellent burrowers. Their front legs are shaped like shovels. This lets them "swim" through the soil. As they burrow, they move nutrients and other organisms. This stops one area from having too many bacteria or fungi.

# SEEDS AND POLLEN

**S**oil is home to plant micro life, too. The surface of soil may be covered with seeds, spores, and pollen from flowers. Some of these can only be seen with a microscope.

## YOU DIG IT

In the fall, see how many different kinds of seeds you can find on the soil in your back yard or local park.

## TINY BEGINNINGS

Seeds come in all sizes and shapes. Most need to be in soil to **germinate**, or sprout. They are carried by the wind, animals, and rain. This helps spread seeds to new areas. Seeds carry with them some food to start growing. Once they sprout and form roots, they take nutrients from the soil. Without enough water and sunlight, they will die.

▼ *Bean plants in the soil*

## TOUGH GUYS

Ferns and fungi use spores to reproduce. They do not have flowers to produce seeds. Each one will produce thousands of spores. Spores do not have stored food to start growing. They can survive in harsh environments for a long time. Once the environment gets better, they begin to grow.

▼ *Spores growing on a fern frond*

▼ *As a bee gets nectar from a cherry flower, it becomes covered in pollen.*

## POLLEN POWER

Pollen is found at the top of the stalk-like **stamens** of flowers. When pollen reaches the upright **pistils** of flowers, seeds are produced. A flower makes a large amount of pollen. Pollen is spread by the wind and by bees and other flying insects. A large amount falls to the ground. Pollen has a tough outer coating. This helps it survive .

## POLLEN FACTS

✳ Pollen can be used as crime evidence. It can prove where a person has been in the countryside. Scientists also study pollen in **fossils**. They can figure out what plants lived in ancient landscapes.

# PEOPLE & MICRO LIFE

People have a huge effect on soil. Chemicals used on crops can kill micro life. Erosion can strip away the top layer of soil. Motorbike trails and sports fields pack soil down too hard. In order to have healthy soil, we need to protect micro life.

▶ *A well-kept back yard will produce a lot of vegetables.*

▲ *Spraying plants in a greenhouse*

## TOO MANY CHEMICALS

Some micro life cause diseases in plants. This is hard for farmers who lose their crops. The artificial chemicals they use to kill the harmful microbes also kill helpful ones. Once micro life has gone, the soil loses its nutrients. Plants need micro life to grow.

## SAVE OUR TREES!

The roots of trees and other plants help hold soil in place. When forests are cut down, the soil is unprotected. Wind and water carry away the top layers of soil. This takes away the home of micro life. Areas can become **barren** and lifeless. The number of trees cut down should be limited.

## YOU DIG IT

It is up to us to help keep our soil healthy. Artificial chemicals should not be used to control pests or weeds or to enrich soil. We should try to use natural methods instead. Grass clippings, leaves, and vegetable peelings can be collected in a compost bin. Organisms in the soil break down these leftovers and create new soil. Composting is a great way to reduce garbage and improve soil. Healthy soil means a healthy planet.

▼ *Put old plant waste in the compost bin.*

# GLOSSARY

**absorb** To take up or take in

**bacteria** Single-celled organisms that break down organic matter

**barren** With very little plant life

**burrow** To dig under ground; also an underground den

**cell** The building block of living things

**chemicals** Natural substances such as carbon or oxygen

**colonies** Groups of the same organism living together

**enzymes** Chemicals that cause a change in matter

**fertile** Rich in nutrients for plant growth

**fossils** The remains of creatures that lived long ago and have turned to rock

**fungi** Living things that live on dead or rotting organic matter

**germinate** A new plant growing from seed

**global warming** A gradual increase in Earth's temperature

**hyphae** The long, thin, hair-like structures produced by fungi such as mushrooms

**larvae** The young of some insects, such as caterpillars

**leguminous** Plants that grow with bacteria that fix nitrogen

**microbes** Microscopic one-celled creatures

**mineral** Any solid inorganic matter

**nutrients** Chemicals that an organism needs to live and grow

**organic** Made from living material

**organisms** Living things

**pistils** The female parts of flowers, which receive pollen

**pollutants** Chemicals that are harmful or poisonous

**protein** A complex chemical used to make cells

**protozoa** Tiny single-celled animals

**reproduce** To have young

**stamens** The male parts of flowers, which produce pollen

**symbiotic** Living together so both organisms benefit

**tiller** A farm tool used to break up the soil

**vibrations** Back and forth motions

# MORE INFORMATION

## FURTHER READING

*Invisible ABC's: Exploring the World of Microbes.* Rodney Anderson. American Society Microbiology, Jan 2007

*Microlife: From Amoebas to Viruses.* Anna Claybourne. Heinemann InfoSearch, Jun 2004

*Dirt: The Ecstatic Skin of the Earth.* Logan, William Bryant. W.W. Norton, 2007.

*Life in a Bucket of Soil.* Silverstein, Alvin. Dover Publications, 2000.

*I Love Dirt!* Ward, Jennifer. Trumpeter, 2008.

*Life Cycle of an Earthworm.* Bobbie Kalman. Crabtree Publishing Company, 2004.

## WEB SITES

**Biology 4 Kids:**
www.biology4kids.com/files/micro_main.html

**Underground Adventure:**
www.fieldmuseum.org/undergroundadventure/index.shtml

**Backyard Nature:**
www.backyardnature.net/index.html

**Soil for Schools:**
www.soil-net.com/legacy/schools/index.htm

**Discovery Education—The Dirt on Soil:**
http://school.discoveryeducation.com/schooladventures/soil/

# INDEX